BUYING A
SECOND-HAND CAR

BUYING A
SECOND-HAND CAR

CONSUMERS' ASSOCIATION

Which? Books are commissioned and researched by
Consumers' Association and published by
Which? Ltd,
2 Marylebone Road, London NW1 4DF
Email address: books@which.net

Distributed by The Penguin Group:
Penguin Books Ltd, 27 Wrights Lane, London W8 5TZ

First edition October 1997
Copyright © 1997 Which? Ltd

British Library Cataloguing in Publication Data
A catalogue record for this book is available from the British Library

ISBN 0 85202 686 2

Buying a Second-hand Car contains information from several *Which?*
publications, including the *Buying a Second-hand Car* Action Pack,
Which? magazine and *Which? Car 1997*. Chapter 9 includes material
from *Ins and Outs of Choosing a Car*, published by RICA.
Acknowledgements Chief CA consultant: Philip Dickins; also David
Button, Caroline Jacobs, Liam McCormack, David Rodwell
For information in the text: *Parker's Car Price Guide*, *What Car?*,
Consumer Reports magazine (USA)

For a full list of Which? books, please write to Which? Books,
Castlemead, Gascoyne Way, Hertford X, SG14 1LH
or access our website at http://www.which.net

Cartoons and cover illustration by David Pattison, Cartoon Partnership
Cover design by Creation Communications
Typeset by Saxon Graphics Ltd, Derby
Printed and bound in Great Britain by Caledonian International Book
Manufacturers, Glasgow

CONTENTS

* in text denotes address at back of book

INTRODUCTION

Buying a second-hand car can be daunting. You will have to deal with the finance, insurance and documentation and decide where to buy the vehicle from, while the prospect of carrying out a technical inspection can send all those who don't know their dipstick from their drive shaft into a tailspin.

Knowing what you want – what you really, really want – is crucial to getting it right. There is no point in buying a gas-guzzling, large-engined car if you would be better off with a supermini. This book helps you to assess the type of vehicle that will suit your lifestyle best, including advice for buyers such as elderly or disabled drivers who may have special needs. It explains how to arrange a professional inspection and empowers those not taking this option to evaluate a car with confidence.

Selling your car can be just as complicated as buying a vehicle. This book guides you through the process – from placing the ad to clinching the deal – and includes expert tips on getting the best price, whether you are selling or buying. Prospective buyers should beware of car crime. It's easy to be swayed by what looks like a bargain, but appearances can be deceptive. The perfect car that you have been eyeing up could turn out to be stolen, 'clocked' or a 'ringer'. This book describes the warning signs to look out for and, if you have been sold a faulty car, how to obtain redress, explaining the laws that protect the consumer.

Buying a Second-hand Car demystifies the terminology of the motor industry, giving even first-time buyers the confidence to feel at home both behind the wheel and under the bonnet. The book also contains tips on cutting running costs and improving security once you have purchased the car of your dreams.

THE COST

1

The cost of a second-hand car can be divided into three separate categories:

- **capital loss** Money swallowed simply by buying and owning the car
- **standing costs** Money spent whether or not you use the car
- **running costs** Money spent directly on keeping the car moving.

You should think about all three types of cost and evaluate how much money will be likely to account for each when deciding how much you can afford.

CAPITAL LOSS

Capital loss is all the money swallowed up in buying a car and, ultimately, selling it. Cars lose their value quite rapidly, particularly ones bought new. By buying used you avoid the big initial loss of value; in fact, it is this rapid initial depreciation that really makes buying used worthwhile.

To get facts and figures on car prices, new, used, retail and trade, you need a price guide. The trade uses its own exclusive guides – *Glass's Guide* and the CAP *Black Book* – which are not available to the public. However, there are several widely available price guides: *Parker's Car Price Guide* and *The Book* from

YEAR	SUFFIX PREFIX	NEW PRICE	A1	GOOD	FAIR	TRADE
Astra 1.4i Merit 3dr Hatchback IG 6						
1991	J	8499	3600	3215	1895	2985
1992	J	8533	3865	3540	2100	3275
1992	K	8580	4235	3895	2310	3615
1993	K	8850	4670	4285	2540	3965
1993	L	9135	5050	4640	2745	4285
1994	L	9380	5545	5095	3015	4705
1994	M	9695	6010	5520	3265	5105
1995	M	9895	6485	5955	3525	5510
1995	N	10095	7040	6465	3825	5980
1996	N	10315	7635	7010	4150	6485
1996	P	10450	8215	7545	4465	6980
1997	P	11045	-	-	-	-

Source: Parker's Car Price Guide

MODEL & YEAR	COST NEW	DEALER RETAIL	PRIVATE SALE	PART EX VALUE	TRADE VALUE	AV MILE	MILE ADJ
Astra 1.4i Merit (60 PS) Hatchback 3dr							
91J	8490	3195	2995	2495	2445	52	3
92J	8530	3395	3295	2795	2745	48	3
92K	8700	3845	3545	3095	2995	43	3
93K	8850	4295	3945	3495	3395	40	3
93L	9130	4495	4295	3795	3695	35	3
94L	9380	5145	4745	4295	4195	29	3
94M	9390	5545	5145	4745	4595	24	3
95M	9790	5995	5695	5345	5195	17	3
95N	9890	6645	6245	5895	5745	12	3
96N	10315	7195	6845	6395	6245	6	3

Source: The Book

What Car? are good examples. All of these guides come out monthly and give brief details about most models of car. As rates change regularly, you should make sure that you obtain the current editions of these guides if you want to get the best deal. For each calendar year in which a car is registered and its registration letter, car price guides list two or three selling prices and a trade price. The suggested prices depend on the car's condition and where it is bought, for example from a dealer or privately. Always refer to the instructions of how to use the guides, as condition classifications can vary from guide to guide. The prices quoted in the guides are rough guidelines only; the mileage that a car has done will, in particular, alter the price being asked.

Opposite, we show how these guides display their prices using the example of the Vauxhall Astra Merit 1.4i three-door hatchback. The 'A1' or 'Dealer retail' prices are those that a car dealership would ask for a car with average mileage and in good condition. If you are considering buying a car from a private owner you should expect to pay no more than the 'good' or 'private sale' price. 'Trade' (*Parker's Car Price Guide*) and 'Part Ex' (*The Book*) are rough guides to the value of a used car to a dealer if you were to trade in your car against one on the forecourt. 'Trade Value' (*The Book*) is the value to a dealer if you were to sell your car outright to him.

It is also useful to do your own research in local and national papers, and in the motoring section of *Exchange & Mart* or similar publications, looking for cars of a similar age and condition.

Should you use savings or borrow the money?

Cold, hard cash

This is not a viable option for most people. But if you are lucky enough to have sufficient amounts of cash, it will always be one of the cheapest ways to buy, even allowing for loss of interest on your savings.

For There is no interest to pay, no monthly repayments and you own the car from the outset.

Against Unfortunately, not an option for most people.

Loans and hire purchase

These two types of scheme work in a similar way, but there are important differences.

Hire purchase (HP) is normally arranged through a car dealer. You'll usually need a deposit of between 10 and 40 per cent of the cost of the car. For many people, this will be covered by the part-exchange value of the car they are trading in. You then pay monthly instalments over an agreed period – typically one to five years. You don't own the car until you make the last payment, though, so the car is not yours to sell during this time. If you fail to make payments, the credit company can, in some circumstances, reclaim the car.

If you're getting a bank or building society loan, you don't need a deposit and you own the car from the outset. Typical repayment periods are one to five years. APRs (annual percentage rates) can vary significantly, so it is worth shopping around. Some weekend newspapers have details of the best loans on offer each week.

For This type of scheme is straightforward and easy to understand. With a loan (but not HP), you own the car from the outset.

Against With HP, you can't sell the car during the repayment period without first settling with the finance company.

Personal contract purchase (PCP) schemes

These schemes have been widely promoted recently. A number of franchised dealers offer them for both new and second-hand cars. PCP schemes are similar to HP, but instead of paying off the whole cost of the car during the repayment period, a chunk of it is deferred. This is known as the MGFV (minimum guaranteed future value), and the amount is fixed at the outset. You also have to agree to a minimum amount of mileage you will do during the period of the contract.

When you enter a PCP contract, you pay a deposit (usually 10 to 40 per cent of the car's value) followed by monthly instalments over the next two or three years. These payments are lower than with other types of finance deal, because you are not paying off any of the MGFV – you just pay interest on it. As with HP, you don't own the car during this phase – the finance company does. When the monthly repayment phase is over, you can either trade in the car for a new one, simply return it or buy the car. The car is yours once you pay the MGFV, plus a small fee. But if this is your intention from the outset, you may be better off using a different type of finance scheme.

For Low monthly repayments are the main appeal, and may enable you to purchase a model that you couldn't

13

otherwise have afforded. If you replace your car every two or three years, a PCP may suit you.

Against You don't own the car during the repayment period and it's easy to get taken in by low monthly repayments when the total cost may be higher than with other forms of finance. Mileage limits may be inconvenient.

The older the better?

You have already made the single most cost-effective decision, simply by deciding to buy a used car rather than a new one. In general, the older the car and the longer you keep it the cheaper the ownership costs will be. However, once a car is over five or six years old the potential saving per year levels off, and you may well find maintenance and repair costs rising.

Balancing economy against reliability, it is a good bet to buy a used car around two years old and replace it after you have owned it for three years.

'Nearly new' cars (usually ex-company and lease cars) are less than a year old and cost much less than they would new. Many will still be covered by a warranty, too. These type of cars are often available at franchised dealers and larger used-car retailers, and are well worth looking out for.

STANDING COSTS

You are obliged to pay certain extra costs in order to keep a car legally on the road.

Tax disc

Whatever the car you buy and however much you use it, it is mandatory for most people to pay the same amount for a **vehicle licence**, or **tax disc**. Exceptions include those who receive the higher rate mobility component of the DLA or the War Pensioners' Mobility Supplement (see Chapter 9) and those who own vehicles over 25 years old (classic cars). For cars, the annual licence costs £145, or you can buy six months' licensing at a time for £79.75 (1997 figures).

Insurance

There is a strong probability that your insurance will cost more than the tax disk. Below we explain how insurers calculate their premiums and what type of cover might suit you best.

Type of car

Cars are grouped by insurers in 1–20 groups according to the insurance risk that they present – the more more powerful a car is and the more costly to repair, the more expensive it will be to insure. If you own a car deemed more likely to be stolen (depending on the model and where you live), this will also push costs up.

For example, a small car with a small engine and readily available spare parts, such as a Ford Fiesta, will be in a low group and should be relatively cheap to insure; a large, powerful car, which could be costly to repair, such as a BMW 535i, will be in a high group and will be much more expensive to insure. So check the **insurance grouping** before you buy (see box below). Better still, check with your insurer (or telephone several insurers) to get a proper quote. If you are below a certain age you may find that insurance companies won't insure you at all for certain cars, especially the more powerful models. *Which?* magazine will give you advice on which companies are worth contacting.

Examples of car groupings

Groups 1–5 Fiat Cinquecento, Ford Fiesta 1.1, Nissan Micra 1.0, Peugeot 106 1.1, Renault Clio 1.2, Vauxhall Corsa 1.2

Groups 6–10 BMW 316, Chrysler Neon 2.0, Citroen ZX 1.4, Ford Escort 1.6, Nissan Almera 1.6, Vauxhall Astra 1.4, Volkswagon Golf 1.4

Groups 11–15 Audi A4 1.8, BMW 320i, Ford Mondeo 2.0, Mercedes C180, Rover 623i, Toyota Corolla 1.6, Vauxhall Vectra 2.0

Groups 16–20 Audi A6 2.6, BMW 535i, Ford Probe, Vauxhall Omega 3.0i, Volkswagen Corrado 2.0

(Data source: CAP *Black Book*)

What else affects insurance costs?
A number of factors determine how high or low your insurance premiums will be. In addition to assessing

the type of car you own and its market value, insurers take into consideration various details including your car usage habits, the number of drivers and where you park the car, your age, sex and occupation and even the post code of the area in which you live.

- Generally, older drivers pay less, athough premiums may start to rise for the over-70s.
- People in low-risk jobs (e.g. teachers and civil servants) usually pay less than those in high-risk occupations, including actors and pub landlords.
- Young men often pay more than women of the same age, as they are considered more of a risk.
- Anyone with a bad claims record or previous driving convictions will face higher rates.
- The more drivers insured on a policy, the costlier it will be. It is cheaper to make people 'named drivers' rather than choosing 'any driver' cover.
- You may pay less if you keep your car in a garage overnight as opposed to on the street.
- Premium are affected by where you live – generally, it is more expensive in urban areas than rural regions. Exact costs are calculated according to your post code.

Which type of cover?

By law, you must have insurance cover before you drive on a public road.

The legal minimum insurance requirement is **third party cover**. This insures you against injury to other people, including your passengers, as well as damage to other people's cars and property. However, not all insurers offer third party cover on its own, and most people take out either **third party, fire and theft** or

17

comprehensive cover. **Third party, fire and theft** also covers you if your car is damaged by fire or if it is stolen. Car theft is alarmingly common, so it makes sense to be insured against this particular risk. Fire damage is less common, but if your car does catch fire the odds are high that it will be a write-off if you are not able to put the fire out immediately.

Comprehensive insurance includes the cover provided by third party, fire and theft policies and adds cover against damage to your own car, even if the accident is your own fault. Comprehensive insurance generally covers you for windscreen and glass damage, and may provide a courtesy car if your own car is not

---

Insurance hints

- You must consider the value of the car you want to buy – this has a bearing on the type of insurance you need to arrange. There is little point in choosing an insurance policy of which the cost outstrips the value of your chosen car.
- For most people, comprehensive cover is the best choice. However, if you are young you may find it too costly, especially if you drive a high-performance car. In this case, opt for third party, fire and theft (it may be worth checking the costs, as comprehensive cover is often only a little more expensive).
- An insurance claim for damage to your car cannot exceed the current market value of your car. So if you are buying a cheap, fairly old used car

---

driveable after an accident. It may also provide a range of other benefits, such as cover against loss or damage to personal possessions and personal accident benefit. However, the benefits provided by such schemes are limited, and they should not be considered a substitute for life, health or personal possessions insurance.

Finding an insurer

Not all insurers provide quotes direct – you may have to go through a broker or other intermediate agency. These are listed in *Yellow Pages* under insurance agents, insurance brokers and insurance consultants.

it may well be worth insuring for third party, fire and theft only.

- Policies tend to be fairly similar, but look out for differences which may be relevant to you. For example, some policies provide a free courtesy car if yours is stolen or badly damaged in an accident, and a number include free legal cover. Some policies charge for extending comprehensive cover if you take your car to Europe – if you go abroad frequently, it could be worthwhile finding an insurer that will not charge extra. A number of insurers give discounts for cars fitted with alarms or immobilisers. If you are a newly qualified driver, some insurance companies will give you a one-year's no-claims discount straight away if you take an intensive training course.

It is worth shopping around for car insurance. You may well be able to save money by haggling – asking an insurer to match the lowest quote you have received from another firm.

If things go wrong

If you have a complaint regarding your insurance, first contact your insurer. Most will have a formal complaints procedure. If you are still dissatisfied with the way your complaint has been handled, you should contact the Insurance Ombudsman Bureau (IOB).* However, a small number of insurers are not part of the IOB scheme. You should then try the Personal Insurance Arbitration Service (PIAS).* As a last resort, you may need to go to court.

RUNNING COSTS

Most motorists have a rough idea of the sort of miles per gallon (mpg) to expect. Though many factors are involved – the car's size, weight, shape, gearing and engine design, for example – we tend to consider cars simply according to their engine size, talking about one-litre cars, 1400cc, 1600cc or two-litre cars, for example.

Fuel consumption

Cars have become considerably more frugal over the past 10 years. You no longer have to go for a very low-powered car to get good fuel consumption. Cars with automatic transmission generally have a fuel consumption of 5–15 per cent higher, depending on the model, while diesels come out tops for fuel economy.

To find out the sort of average mpg you should expect from a car you are interested in, check the test reports in *Which?* or in motoring magazines.

You can also check the official fuel consumption test results approved by the Department of Transport. These tests are conducted under ideal conditions, but do nonetheless allow some comparison between cars. The figures are available in some car magazines and car price guides. However, care should be used when comparing these figures since the test method has recently been revised, and not all car manufacturers are using the same method. The new method is claimed to be more realistic and representative of real-life driving but is not directly comparable to the older test method.

Spares and servicing

Petrol is almost certainly the biggest single running expense, but spares and servicing can also be costly. Broadly speaking, popular 'bread-and-butter' cars – Fords, Rovers, Vauxhalls – have relatively inexpensive spares. Relatively low-selling cars, particularly expensive ones, tend to have costly spares. Don't get caught out by buying a big prestige car relatively cheap second-hand only to find you can't afford the cripplingly expensive spares or servicing. How easily you can find spares also depends on how substantial a share of the spares market a car has. This is affected not only by car sales figures but by how long a car has been on sale.

You may find getting spares for a newly introduced car, even one you are buying used, difficult.

When you are checking a particular car note what size and make of tyres have been fitted – unusual ones (for example, fat, low-profile ones) can be very expensive indeed.

Consider the cost of routine servicing and remember that every few years a major service may be required that involves more expensive items such as a cam belt change. Also get an idea of the cost of 'wear and tear' parts; brake pads and discs, and an exhaust system. For more on how to reduce your running costs, see Chapter 8.

WHAT FEATURES TO GO FOR

2

You have probably already made up your mind about what basic size and body style of car you want. This chapter goes over some further points that are worth considering, and describes how to choose a car with specifications suited to your needs.

BIG OR SMALL?

If you are buying new, the size of car you choose will be determined to a large extent by how much money you have. The effects of depreciation, though, mean that a used-car buyer will discover that cars of all different sizes are within his or her budget. As a general rule, the bigger a car is, the safer it will be in a crash. But larger cars are likely to cost more to insure, refuel and get serviced and repaired. Smaller cars can be easier to re-sell, too. Below we summarise the pros and cons of common body styles.

Saloons

- generally offer rather more security for luggage than estates or hatchbacks
- may have a high boot sill – which can be awkward for loading luggage.

Estates

- offer the most practical load-carrying volume – the back end is usually fairly square and upright
- can cope with heavy or bulky loads
- almost invariably have a low back sill – good for getting heavy things in and out of the back
- can leave your luggage vulnerable – a temptation to the light-fingered.

Hatchbacks

- are less practical load-carriers than estates but better than saloons
- mostly have a fairly high back sill – which means that they are less easy to load than an estate
- mostly have a hinged back shelf, covering luggage when the back seat is up.

Coupés

- may provide you with back seats, but don't expect anyone other than small children to fit in – most cars of this design are very cramped in the back
- are often considerably more costly but perform little or no more sportily than roomier saloons or hatchbacks in the same range.

Two or four passenger doors?

Two doors are:

- usually cheaper than their four-door equivalents
- often awkward for back-seat passengers.

Four-doors are:

- much more convenient for back passengers and for loading up hatchbacks or estates
- fitted with safety catches on the back doors: as long as you remember to set the catch, children should be safe and unable to open the doors from inside the car.

ENGINE SIZE AND TYPE

Should you go for a big engine (over 2000cc, say) or not? The general guidelines for cars are straightforward enough. The bigger the engine:

- the more powerful
- the more thirsty
- the more expensive the car.

If economy is your main concern, go for a smallish-engined car, but not one that is clearly under-powered. A good engine size for small hatchbacks (or 'superminis') is around 1200cc; the equivalent for family saloons and hatchbacks is around 1400cc. You are better off buying a smaller, more frugal car than buying a big 'gas-guzzler' and then trying to run it economically.

If engine power and performance are your chief concerns you are probably better off with a larger engine option. A larger car and engine are essential if you want to tow a caravan or trailer. Ask yourself, however, exactly why you want more power – is it going to be worth the greater running expenses?

25

Diesel-powered cars

Diesel-powered cars have had a reputation for being slow, noisy and smelly – not a good choice for a pleasant family car. This may have been true at one point in time, but diesel cars – and their image – have been changing over the last few years, and now you can get a diesel version of many of the most popular models of car.

Diesel-powered cars are still generally rather slower than equivalent petrol-engined cars, but not embarrassingly so, however. Some are noisy when ticking over, but once you are on the move this is less noticeable. Diesel-powered cars are not particularly smelly, though diesel fuel does not evaporate as easily as petrol and so may linger longer – this is often noticeable at the fuel pumps.

Diesel cars are certainly more economical on fuel than equivalent-powered petrol cars. However, they do tend to cost a bit more than petrol-engined cars to buy and you are only likely to end up better off overall if you drive a large number of miles each year.

Transmission

Cars with automatic transmission (which make the necessity of changing gear redundant) tend to use a bit more petrol than those with manual transmission, are usually more expensive to buy and often don't perform as well as manual transmission cars. You may feel, however, that these drawbacks are outweighed by the easier and more relaxed driving that automatic transmission can offer, especially on big, family saloons.

OTHER FEATURES

There are some other aspects of car design that you should take into consideration.

Safety is now considered a major selling point by car manufacturers, and it features heavily in car advertisements these days. Special features such as airbags and side-impact bars are now standard on a wide range of models. There is, however, more to safety than special features. *Which?* has been testing cars for secondary safety – how well they will protect you in a crash – since the early 1980s. Tests take into account different types of accident, from front-on crashes to roll-over accidents, and look at how much protection occupants would have. *Which? Car** publishes details of the ratings for various models.

A major advance in improving car safety recently occurred with the establishment of the Euro NCAP crash-test programme for new cars. Results of initial tests on superminis showed that more development is needed on driver's airbags. Researchers in the United States have found that unrestrained children in the front seat and babies in rear-facing seats in the front could be at risk from inflating air bags, as could short adults.

- If your car is fitted with airbags, it is still important to both wear a seat belt yourself and also to ensure that children belt up – anyone too small to wear lap-and-shoulder belts properly should ride in the rear.
- Drivers should stay as far back from the steering wheel as possible, ideally 12 inches away, and con-

sider pedal extenders if sitting this far away prevents them from reaching the pedals (see Chapter 9 for information on car adaptations).

● Never mount a rear-facing infant or child seat in the front seat of a car with a passenger-side airbag.

Car security has seen significant improvement in recent years. You should consider security features such as engine immobilisers and alarms: if the car you have chosen does not come with these as standard you may wish to add them as 'after market' devices. Older cars (those more than five years old) are more popular with thieves these days – they are seen as 'soft targets', because they are so much easier to break into and steal than newer models.

Modern cars come with a wide range of **convenience features** such as power steering, sunroofs, central locking and electric windows. These may be part of your requirements, but do not pay over the odds for extra features. Also, if buying an 'executive'-class car beware of buying one with low equipment levels as the car may be difficult to sell when you eventually decide to change it.

Which car for you?

Once you have decided your price limit and what sort of car would most suit your needs, you are well on your way to your own shortlist of likely cars. Motoring magazines and car reports in *Which?* are a useful source of general information and driving impressions of different models. Every June, *Which?* produces a car-buying guide, with details on both current production cars and popular cars now out of production. This also includes reliability information; a major consideration when buying a car. The *Which? Car** guide is only available to *Which?* subscribers, but can be consulted at public libraries.

Selling Your Car 3

First, make sure the car is yours to sell. If you bought the car with a hire purchase or conditional sale agreement (where you pay in instalments), the car is owned by the finance company, so you can't sell it until all payments have been made. Also, any car being sold must be in a roadworthy condition – whether or not it has an MOT certificate – unless you're selling it for parts or scrap.

The best sales method

Selling privately, using an ad in a paper or magazine, will usually get you the best price but you will need to put in quite a lot of effort.

Selling to a dealer usually won't yield as much money as a private sale, particularly in the quiet months from October to December and in July (prior to the August trade-ins), but it is usually quick. Part-exchange through a dealer should give you a better trade-in price, but the dealer may then not offer you as big a discount on the car you are buying from them. Get a feel for the average trade-in price of your car by checking a monthly car price guide.

An auction (see Chapter 4) will not get you as much as a private sale, but it can be quick and is at arm's length. Put a reserve price on your car if there is a minimum amount you will accept.

Setting the price

To find out the value of your car, check a monthly car price guide (see Chapter 1). To attract buyers, you will need to undercut the highest prices listed in these publications for your model and age of car. Have a look at the prices of cars in newspaper and magazine ads to get a feel for what's around. Set yourself a minimum price that you will accept – private sales in particular are likely to involve haggling.

Where to advertise

The best way to advertise depends on the make and model of your car. If you own a popular model, such as a Ford Escort, it is best to advertise in a local paper

31

because buyers will not be prepared to travel far. If the car isn't worth much (under £500, say), try a card in a local newsagent or a supermarket noticeboard.

With a prestige or collector's car, you should consider advertising in a national newspaper or car magazine. Some makes and models – VW Beetles, Citroen 2CVs and MGs – have specialist newsletters and magazines.

Placing the ad

As well as your car's make and model, it is important to include the year or registration letter. It is also worth giving the month of registration if it was late in the year – e.g. June or July. Give the colour and mention any special features, such as a sun roof or low mileage. Say what condition the vehicle is in and mention if you can provide a full service history for the car. Finally, give the price and your contact number.

PREPARING YOUR CAR

To improve the chances of getting the best price for your car:

- get an MOT done if it's due and you think the car will pass
- give the car a thorough clean inside and out
- empty the boot
- prepare the paperwork – garage service invoices and service booklet, handbook, Vehicle Registration Document (V5) and MOT certificate.

Allow a potential buyer plenty of time, and don't talk too much.

Don't misrepresent your car

Legally, the car must be 'as described'. For example, if you say in your ad that the car is in excellent condition even though it isn't, you may be liable for misrepresentation, and could be forced to give the buyer their money back. You should always answer questions honestly because you can be sued if you lie about the car.

If you make any agreements – that you will supply accessories such as seat covers or a stereo, or that you will have a fault fixed before the sale, for example – make sure that you stick to them. If you don't, you are in breach of contract, and could be sued by the buyer.

Test drive

If you are willing to let prospective buyers test-drive your car, make sure that your insurance – or theirs – covers any driver. Most people do not have comprehensive cover, so if another person causes an accident while driving your car, you are the one that could be out of pocket. For more on insurance, see Chapter 1.

Finalising the sale

Don't hand over the car or its documents until you have received cleared funds. It is possible that the form of payment could be forged.

If you are given a banker's draft or a building society cheque, ask for the phone number and address of the branch it was drawn from so that you can check that everything is *bona fide*.

33

With a bank cheque, wait until it has cleared your account before handing over the car keys.

GETTING READY TO BUY

Having decided what car you want, you need to track down likely examples. You have three possible sources.

BUYING FROM A GARAGE OR CAR DEALER

'Shop around' is the best advice. You *may* spot the car of your dreams on a local dealer's forecourt, but it usually pays to spread your net wider. Look in your local newspaper – these usually carry plenty of ads, listing local dealers' stocks. This method can also be a short-cut to finding a dealer in your area who specialises in particular makes of car in which you are interested. You can look even further afield by poring over a specialist car-ad magazine such as *AutoTrader* or the motoring section of *Exchange & Mart*.

It is well worth buying a car-ad magazine, not just for particular ads but also to get a general idea of what is on the market and what sort of prices people are asking. Beware of the unscrupulous dealer, advertising cars in small ads as if from a private address – he may be tidying up poor-condition cars and passing them off as genuine private sales, thus limiting your legal protection. This is illegal – inform your local Trading Standards Officer if you come across a dealer doing this. The Business Advertisement (Disclosure) Order 1977 requires that ads make it clear if someone is selling in the course of business. Many publications and newspapers put the symbol 'T' next to business ads.

Advantages
- You have better legal protection under the Sale of Goods Act 1979 (as amended by the Sale and Supply of Goods Act 1994).
- You may get a guarantee of some sort, which can take the heat out of problems after you've bought the car.
- The car will probably be clean and not have any obvious defects.
- You will be able to inspect the car carefully and take it for a test drive.
- There will be no hassles with previous ownership.
- You may be offered a part-exchange deal for a car you are selling.

Disadvantages
- This is not the cheapest way to buy – top prices will be asked.
- You may feel pressurised into buying a car by the salesman.

Verdict
Buying from a reputable dealer is sensible if you don't know very much about cars – you are paying extra for a safer deal. Take your time and do not be pressurised into making a quick decision.

BUYING FROM AN AUCTION

Once almost exclusively the stamping-ground of dealers, car auctions are now trying more and more to attract private buyers, too. There are bargains to be had, but you need your wits about you. Bear in mind the following points if you fancy a flutter (it really can be a gamble).

Advantages
- Prices at auction will almost certainly be lower than buying from a dealer or privately.
- It is very quick.

Disadvantages
- You have virtually no chance to test a car – you more or less buy 'on spec'.
- Many cars, particularly older ones, are sold 'as seen' or 'with all faults as found'. This means you have no comeback if things go wrong.
- If anything *is* wrong with the car you have little chance of getting much done.
- You have little chance to find out anything about the car's history.
- You probably won't get a guarantee or warranty unless the car is fairly new; even then this warranty is limited.
- Bidding is not a game for novices. You may, for example, in one scenario end up bidding against only one other bidder at an auction, unaware that he or she is in actual fact the seller, bumping up the price.

Verdict

Buying a car at an auction is very risky, even if you know what you are doing. This method is not to be recommended.

BUYING PRIVATELY

People selling their own cars privately tend to advertise by placing small ads in local newspapers, newsagents or in the same specialist magazines that dealers use.

Advantages

- A private sale should be cheaper than buying from a dealer.
- You should have a good chance to check the car over carefully and take it for a test drive.
- You have a fair chance of learning at least some of the car's past history.

Disadvantages

- You have little legal redress if things go wrong, although the car should 'correspond with the description' as a second-hand car, and any statements made about it must be correct. So take a witness along, and keep the original advertisement if it contains a description of the car.
- You have no voluntary protection, e.g. a guarantee.

Verdict

A private buy is sensible if you have some knowledge of cars and are buying on a tight budget.

What to do before viewing

It is well worth doing some background work and carrying out a bit of simple research before you go to view a possible buy. Make a short list of things that you have already learnt about the model of car – for example, likely fuel consumption, servicing and routine maintenance costs, insurance grouping and the sort of prices quoted in guides for the car's age and mileage – or any other useful facts that you may have gleaned from studying lots of ads. Try to find two or three examples of car that you would like to view – do not limit yourself to just one car.

You can get a lot of useful information from the *Which? Car** guide, available every June; in particular, what weak spots have been revealed in various models. The *Which? Car* guide publishes a survey that covers the most popular models of car.

It's a good idea to check a map of the area around the seller – for the road test you will need quiet roads, and, ideally, a stretch of fast dual carriageway.

You should be aware of your legal rights as a buyer. See Chapter 7 for a simple guide to possible pitfalls and the protection available to protect the consumer.

Be prepared

If you intend to check over the car yourself, wear old clothes, or take some overalls – you will probably be likely to get oil or dirt on your clothes. Also, arrange for someone knowledgeable to come along with you, to discuss points with, to witness any claims the seller makes and simply to be a second pair of eyes. For details of how to get a car professionally inspected, see Chapter 5.

Be equipped

You don't need a bulging toolbox, but a few things will be useful:

- a screwdriver, for prodding and poking suspect rusty areas
- a tyre-tread depth gauge to check the tyres properly
- a torch to shine into dark corners and underneath the car
- cleaning rags with which to wipe the dipstick, and your hands when they get dirty
- a notebook and pen for recording vehicle condition and other important details.

Checking a car

If, like most people, you are not accustomed to checking used cars, it is easy to miss a serious defect. Use the lists on the following pages for a systematic approach.

Getting the car inspected

If you are not confident about checking a car you are interested in yourself, and don't know someone who can check it for you, you may wish to pay for a professional inspection. Most of these are performed by local assessors but some breakdown organisations, including the AA,* carry them out, too. They aren't cheap – costs range from £75 to £300, depending on the inspection company and the type of car – but they may save you money in the long run. You will normally be supplied with a written report and the price may also include an HPI or CCN check, too (see box). It is worth noting that inspection reports which point out defects with the car can also strengthen your hand when it comes to negotiating a fair price for the vehicle.

Paperwork

It is vital to check the vehicle's documentation carefully. The most important piece of paper is the Vehicle Registration Document, or V5. Accept no excuses where the V5 is concerned. If you are buying second-

Car check

A number of companies gather data on used cars that can be accessed by the general public. To find out if a car you are seriously considering is subject to outstanding hire purchase payments, is a registered write-off, or has been stolen, you should call HPI* or CCN* to check whether it is on their database. An HPI enquiry costs £28.50, and one from CCN £25 (£19.50 if you're an AA* member). However, sometimes an HPI check is included in the price of a professional used-car inspection.

Running this kind of check is not a cast-iron guarantee that everything is OK, as these companies' data is only as comprehensive as the information they are supplied with by finance companies, insurers and the police – but it will be money well spent if it shows up a serious problem. If you are buying from a dealer ask whether the vehicle has already been checked out with HPI or CCN.

hand or privately, the vendor's name and address should be on the top of the V5 document. If it is a private sale and the seller's name isn't on it or the address is wrong, steer clear. The car may not belong to the person selling it, or the vendor may be a dealer posing as a private seller. Likewise, if the person selling the car can't produce the V5, give the vehicle a wide berth. Even if the reason for a discrepancy is legitimate, the risk isn't worth taking.

The ideal car is one with a full service history, a full set of MOT certificates (if over three years old) and receipts for all services and repairs.

- Try to contact previous owners to verify a car's mileage. Ask them what the mileage was when they sold the car – this way you will be able to tell if the car has been clocked or not (see 'Clocking', Chapter 5).
- Check that the mileages recorded in the service book tally with those on MOT certificates and correspond with the odometer (mileage recorder) reading.
- Check whether documents look suspiciously new or old, or the service book is complete.
- If you're buying from a dealer, ask if they have tried to verify the car's mileage – they have to by law.
- Be very wary if the mileage is being disclaimed by a dealer by means of a sticker next to the odometer. This may mean that they were unable legitimately to verify a car's mileage. But it could mean that they know the mileage is wrong and want to avoid prosecution.

Whether you are buying from a dealer or privately, it is worth asking the seller a lot of questions and giving the car a thorough check.

THINGS TO ASK THE SELLER

- Do you have the receipt that you got when you bought the car? (There is no need to ask this of a dealer.) Possessing a Vehicle Registration Document (the V5) is not necessarily proof of ownership.

43

TYPICAL PETROL-ENGINED CAR LAYOUT

1 Vehicle Identification Number (VIN) plate
2 'Stamped in' Vehicle Identification Number (VIN)
3 Body Panels
4 Box-sections
5 Sills
6 Wheel arches
7 Exhaust system
8 Exhaust catalyst
9 Fuel tank
10 Spare tyre
11 Front shock absorbers or dampers
12 Brake pipes and hoses
13 Clutch housing
14 Battery
15 Gearbox
16 Drive shafts
17 Brake discs and calipers

18 Alternator
19 Radiator and cooling fan
20 Distributor
21 Ignition leads
22 Engine coolant reservoir
23 Brake fluid reservoir and master cyl
24 Spark plugs
25 Dipstick
26 Oil filter cap
27 Headlights
28 Sidelights
29 Number plate lights
30 Stop lights
31 Fog lights
32 Indicators
33 Reversing lights
34 Wipers and washers

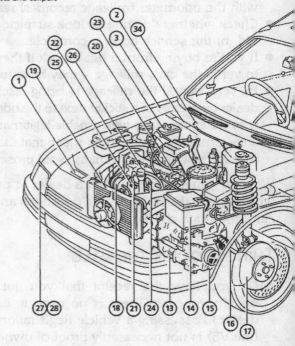

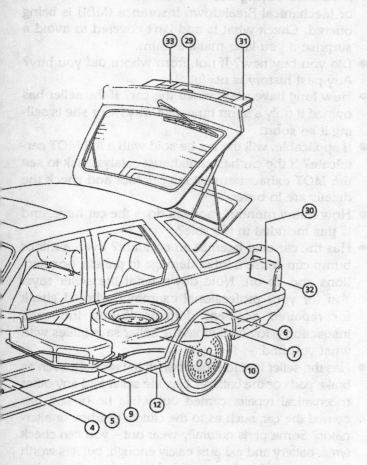

- If you are buying from a dealer, ask what warranty or Mechanical Breakdown Insurance (MBI) is being offered. Check what is and isn't covered to avoid a surprise if you later make a claim.
- Did you buy new? If not, from whom did you buy? Any past history is useful.
- How long have you owned the car? If the seller has owned it only a short time, ask why he or she is selling it so soon.
- If applicable, will the car be sold with a full MOT certificate? If the car has an exhaust catalyst, ask to see the MOT exhaust emissions printout and check the details are in order.
- How many months' road tax does the car have, and is this included in the sale?
- Has the car ever been in an accident? Even a minor bump can cause a lot of damage to panels, box-sections and so on. Note down what the seller says. You (or your professional examiner) should check for repaired accident damage during the car's inspection – to see if what the seller says tallies with what you find.
- Has the seller had to replace anything recently, such as brake pads or the battery? Has the seller had any other mechanical repairs carried out while he or she has owned the car, such as to the clutch, gearbox or alternator? Some parts naturally wear out – you can check tyres, battery and exhaust easily enough, but it is worth knowing whether inaccessible bits such as the brakes or clutch have had attention, and at what mileage.
- Take notes of what the seller says.

Clocking

Investigations have shown that 'clocking' is still amaz-ingly commonplace. 'Clocking' is the popular name for resetting a car's mileage recorder to a lower figure, or zero, and is illegal if it is done deliberately to mis-lead a buyer. A 'clocked' car is not always easy to detect. The only way may be to check back with pre-vious owners. Failing that, you simply have to rely on what you can learn from the car's general condition. Worn pedal rubbers, carpets and seat covers, a shiny gear knob and steering wheel, as well as excessive paint chipping on the front of the car, may all point to a high-mileage car.

CHECKING THE CAR

Having quizzed the seller, you (or your professional examiner) should now thoroughly check the car.

Don't let the seller take the lead, showing you what he or she wants you to see and brushing over things about which he or she is less confident. Don't be tempted to leap into the car, start the engine and sail off around the block.

The main areas of the inspection, mostly visual, are as follows. A professional examiner will go into more detail.

Vehicle Identification Number

You should start by checking that the documentation matches the car. The Vehicle Registration Document or

V5 carries a 17-digit Vehicle Identification Number (VIN). This number is also on the vehicle on a plate and stamped into the body – some cars have the VIN on the fascia also. (The diagram on pages 44 and 45 shows a typical layout of a petrol-engined car and the position of the VIN, although this varies from model to model – consult the vehicle handbook or a dealer if in doubt.)

'Ringing' is when a criminal gives a stolen car a new identity by swapping its documents and VIN plates with those of a 'donor' car. The donor is usually an accident-damaged write-off. If you buy a 'ringer', you don't legally own it. You can avoid this by carrying out a careful inspection.

Check that:

- the VIN plate has not been interfered with or removed
- the stamping in the body is even and that the surrounding bodywork has not been altered or interfered with
- the engine number, on the engine block, matches that given on the Vehicle Registration Document (V5)
- the registration number matches any window etchings of the registration number or VIN.

The full VIN is not always used in any window etching. If you are in any doubt or there are inconsistencies, it is best to steer clear and find another suitable car; the vehicle you are looking at may be stolen. If you are at all suspicious, it is a good idea to see whether the car is on either the HPI or CCN registers (see 'Car check' box, page 42).

During your inspection, try to decide whether or not the car's condition reflects its indicated or declared mileage.

On top of the car

Before you check underneath the car, while it is on the ground and not on a lift, make sure that the doors, boot and bonnet are closed. Walk around the vehicle checking for any irregularities in panel gaps which may indicate poor crash repairs. Similarity, check bumpers for areas of poor fit and paint damage. You should also check paint colour match between panels. The car should be clean and dry and positioned in a reasonable light source (not necessarily bright sunlight) for this exercise to be carried out properly. Again, poor paint match indicates accident damage and possibly poor-quality crash repairs. Look down along each side of the car at an acute angle: this will help to show up poor panel fit and damage.

Also check for:

- stone chipping and dents
- paint overspray on door and window seals, indicating body repairs and respray
- doors, boot and bonnet all open, close and lock properly
- tyre damage e.g. cuts, splits and bulges. Check the spare if it is in the boot and make sure there is a jack and wheel-changing tools. (Don't forget the device to unlock locking wheel nuts, if these are fitted)
- wheel and trim damage

- lights, including indicators, brake and reversing lights should operate correctly and lenses should not be broken or cracked
- correct shock absorbers or damper operation (push down firmly and release each corner of the car in turn). The car should bounce up and return immediately to its normal position. If it continues to bounce up and down this indicates weak or worn shock absorbers or dampers.

Underneath the car

The part of the body of a car that gets the least attention is the underside. If you are buying from a dealer, ask him to put the car on a lift and leave you to look around. If you are buying privately you will probably have to do your best on the ground. Do not rely on a car jack alone if you want to get a better look at the underside of the vehicle – use additional supports such as ramps or axle stands.

Make notes of what you find; these will come in handy when considering several cars or when haggling over the price. On cars that are under 6–8 years old, rust and corrosion should not be too much of a problem. Some surface rusting in certain areas and on some components may be evident even on fairly new cars. Pay more attention to possible corrosion on older cars, particularly on the wheel arches, along the sills, box sections and floor areas. Use a screwdriver to check and prod any suspect areas, but remember, it's not your car yet! Severe corrosion in structural areas can lead to a vehicle failing the MOT test and can be expensive to repair.

Whilst underneath the car check for:

- any areas of body damage or poor repair
- corrosion and holes in the exhaust system
- excessive rust/corrosion and signs of brake fluid leakage on brake pipes, brake drums or brake calipers
- split brake hoses; excessive scoring/pitting of brake discs
- fuel tank and fuel pipe leakage; excessive corrosion/rust
- excessive wear of brake pads and shoes (if visible)
- engine oil or fluid leaks; gearbox oil leaks
- drive shaft damage; splitting of rubber boots
- steering rack fluid leaks (on power assisted steering –

PAS – systems); damage or splitting of rubber boots
- damaged suspension components; splitting or cracking of suspension rubber mountings
- fluid leaks around shock absorbers or dampers
- tyre-tread depth and signs of damage e.g. cuts, splits and bulges; uneven wear (tyres with less than 2mm will need changing soon if not immediately). Check the spare if it is mounted underneath the car
- wheel rim damage
- rust, dents or damage to the lower part of all body panels.

Under the bonnet

Use our diagram on pages 44–5 to familiarise yourself with the typical layout, if necessary. Conduct the initial inspection with the engine switched off and take care around moving parts when it is running.

Check for:

- signs of corrosion, particularly upper suspension mountings, on older cars
- correct fluid levels of engine oil, brake fluid, engine coolant and PAS – Power Assisted Steering – fluid (if applicable). If the vehicle has been recently serviced, the engine oil should be either reasonably clear or light brown in colour. Heavy black colouring, particularly on petrol-engined cars, indicates that an engine oil change is required.
- engine oil and coolant leakages
- radiator corrosion and leakage
- brake fluid leakage

- signs of corrosion around the battery (even on newer cars) and the battery terminals.

Start the engine and check for:

- ease of engine starting and smoothness of running whilst cold
- excessive engine smoke from the exhaust whilst revving the engine
- strange noises e.g. knocking or grinding sounds.

Inside the car and behind the wheel

Now that you have gone through the major mechanical and bodywork checks you can get on with the more straightforward matter of the state of the car's interior. Unless you are already familiar with the model, you'll probably find yourself absorbed by the novelty of an 'unknown' car and possibly swayed by its appearance. Try to remain objective: maybe the seats, the radio or the controls are terrific, but don't allow your judgement to be distorted by appealing features and non-essentials.

Check the following:

- condition of interior trim, carpets, seats and roof lining
- apparent wear of steering wheel, pedals and other controls
- operation of wipers and washers, heater fan, radio cassette player/compact disc player and any other equipment
- operation of windows and sunroof
- assess cracks and chipping of windscreen
- operation and condition of seat belts.

53

Decide for yourself whether or not you are happy with the condition of the interior of the car and whether it reflects the car's claimed mileage. Some unscrupulous sellers will tamper with a car's mileage recorder to give the impression that the car has done less than is really the case (see 'Clocking', above).

THE ROAD TEST

If you are happy with your inspection so far and you consider the car to be safe, the next step is a road test. Make sure that you are covered by insurance before driving on public roads (see Chapter 1).

If you are an experienced driver you will no doubt soon spot any serious problems that affect the controls and response of the car. Here are a few points to remember as you do your checks:

- Some cars have inherently poor gear selection, so a poor gear change may not actually be faulty. You should, however, consider whether a mediocre gear change is something with which you can live.
- When carrying out checks on brakes, check behind you *and* warn any passengers in the car that you are going to brake.
- If you can't do a hill test, don't worry. Handbrake problems are usually a matter of adjustment and are not too expensive to remedy. You can check the clutch at the end of the road test – if it's not engaging as soon as you release it, or slipping, the clutch linings could be worn and will need replacing.
- Steering vibration is rarely a major problem. Often,

simple wheel balancing will correct any problem.
- Braking problems obviously have serious safety implications, but generally speaking are not too difficult to resolve.

While performing a road test check the following:

- operation and smoothness of engine, brakes, steering and gear change, including clutch
- unusual noises e.g. rattles, squeaks and clunks.

After the road test

Check under the bonnet for the presence of fluid leaks and rev the engine to make sure that it runs normally and smoothly. Also check for engine smoke from the exhaust and for any unusual noises while revving the engine.

Make sure you understand how security features such as immobilisers and alarms work. In addition, make sure that all the keys are available, including master keys associated with cars that have factory fitted immobilisers – if in doubt, consult the vehicle handbook or a franchised dealer.

CLOSING THE DEAL

Once you have found the car that you would like to buy, preferably after looking at several examples, the next step is to close the deal.

AGREEING A PRICE

The main bone of contention when buying a second-hand car may well turn out to be agreeing the price with the seller. If, after you (or your professional examiner) have thoroughly checked the car, you consider the price to be reasonable, then there is no problem and you can proceed with the sale. But if the seller is asking the top price and you have discovered that you are going to need to spend £300 on new tyres, a brake overhaul or new dampers, you would be entitled to question the 'first-class' price that the seller is asking.

Armed with your checklists and estimates of repair, adjustment or replacement costs, you should be in a good position to negotiate a more realistic price.

If the seller won't budge, start looking for another possible buy. As a buyer of a used car, you should no more accept the cost of defects than the buyer of a new car, who expects the maker to fix faults under a guarantee.

You may find that the seller suggests 'putting right' defects before handing over the car. Be wary of this. There is little incentive for him or her to do more than the minimum job, particularly if you have already committed yourself to buy. The answer is not to commit yourself. You can either hold out for a sensible price reduction or offer to re-check the car if the seller does decide to put faults right. But don't part with your money on the strength of a promise that 'the steering will be overhauled' before you pick the car up, for example.

If the car has removable accessories – e.g. radio, speakers, seat covers – ask the seller to clarify what is included in the sale.

Do not pay for the car using large amounts of cash. A banker's draft is safer.

PAPERWORK

You will need:

- A signed and dated receipt for the deal as proof of payment, making it clear that you have paid such-and-such an amount of money and are now the owner of the car.
- The Vehicle Registration Document (the V5). The seller must fill in and send off the tear-off slip at the bottom of this document. And you, the buyer, must fill in and send off the top part.
- A valid MOT certificate if the car is three or more years old.
- Insurance – at least a cover note from your insurance company.
- Any guarantee paperwork: in addition to whatever a dealer may offer as a sale incentive, more and more manufacturers are offering long-term guarantees,

particularly for corrosion. This is worth knowing about and could, if necessary, be worth trying as a first step if something goes wrong. But if these guarantees have required the owner to stick to a strict schedule of checks, ask for proof that these have been carried out, otherwise the guarantee really is worthless. Study the wording of the guarantee carefully: some guarantees offer very limited cover and carry extensive exclusions.

- Ask the seller for any service records, receipts and vehicle handbooks.

Tracing a car's history

You may well want to know more about a car's past. The old-style log book, phased out in the 1970s, used to provide a record of all previous registered owners. You can still get this information, but only if you are now the registered owner. Write to the Non-fee-paying Enquiry Section at the Driver Vehicle and Licensing Authority (DVLA).*

WHAT TO DO IF THINGS GO WRONG

Despite the best-laid plans, when buying a car there is always a possibility that you might end up with a dud. Fortunately, laws exist to protect the consumer which you might be able to call on to ameliorate the situation if this happens to you.

What if the seller was still buying on hire purchase?

The majority of major items today are bought on hire purchase. If you buy goods on HP, the goods remain the property of the hire purchase company until the final payment has been made. So if you buy goods not knowing that they are subject to an HP agreement, the hire purchase company will be able to reclaim them from you.

Cars are an exception to this rule. If you buy a car from someone who hasn't finished paying off hire purchase payments, you will none the less become the lawful owner provided you can prove that you are the *first* private buyer of the car *and* that you didn't know the car was subject to hire purchase agreement. This is laid down in Part III of the Hire Purchase Act 1964.

This exception applies even if you buy a used car subject to a hire purchase agreement from a dealer who, in turn, had bought it from the hirer. Since a dealer is a trade buyer he does not have Part III protection, even if he buys for his own private use. The original buyer of the car on HP is, of course, still responsible for his or her debt.

There is an organisation called HP Information Limited who register hire purchase agreements. Although HP Information Limited is a members' organisation, it makes its information available to the AA,* RAC* and Citizens Advice Bureaux. So if you are considering buying a used car, you would be strongly advised to find out first whether the car is subject to an HP agreement. Remember, Part III of the Hire Purchase Act protects only the first private buyer in the chain.

What if the car turns out to be stolen or subject to a lease agreement?

You should always remember that the registered keeper of a car is not necessarily the legal owner. If you buy a car that has been stolen, or one that is subject to a leasing agreement, you will have no legal title to it. Since the seller was not the true owner of the car, he or she had no legal right to sell it and cannot transfer ownership to you.

The original owner remains the rightful owner throughout and is legally entitled to demand the car back. If you refuse to return the car, the original owner will be entitled to bring a claim against you for either the return of the car or its value.

But you are not without a remedy. Under the Sale of Goods Act (as amended), your seller made an implied promise that he or she owned the car and that owner-ship of the car would pass to you on its sale. You are therefore entitled to recover the price you paid for the car from your seller. It is irrelevant that your seller had no knowledge or suspicion that the car was stolen: the implied promise imposes *strict* liability on any seller.

What if a car you bought directly from a dealer is faulty or not as described?

When you buy a second-hand car from a dealer, you enter into a contract with him governed by the Sale of Goods Act 1979 (as amended). Under the Sale and Supply of Goods Act 1994, the car must be of 'satis-factory quality', which means that the car should be fit

for its purpose – i.e. driving – free from minor defects, safe and durable. Whether a second-hand car is of satisfactory quality depends on its description, age and the price you paid for it. If the car is not of satisfactory quality, the dealer is in breach of contract and you can claim compensation as outlined below.

The Sale of Goods Act also states that the car must correspond with any description given of it at the time it was sold to you. If you can show that your car didn't meet these requirements at the time of sale, you would have a claim against the dealer for breach of contract.

The dealer, however, will not be responsible if he draws certain defects of the car to your attention before you buy. Neither will the dealer be responsible if, before you buy, you or your own professional examiner check the car and fail to spot problems that a reasonable inspection ought to have revealed. Obviously, there will be cases where an examination is not going to reveal a latent defect. The position in this case is that the dealer will still be responsible – provided, of course, that you can prove that the defect existed at the time of sale.

If you have a complaint regarding a car you have purchased from a dealer, here is a step-by-step guide to follow.

Step one
Find out if your complaint is legally justified. You should remember that the onus rests on you to prove your case, so it is worth getting an expert's report on the car's faults. An organisation like the AA* or RAC* may be able to help you. Alternatively, the Institute of

Automotive Engineer Assessors* will provide the names of independent engineers.

You should also consider obtaining legal advice. You can get free legal advice from Citizens Advice Bureaux, Law Centres and Consumer Advice Centres. Some solicitors offer a fixed-fee interview.

Step two

To avoid losing any legal rights that you may have, you will need to act quickly. If the car is clearly inherently defective and you no longer want it, you should contact the seller immediately and notify him or her of your claim. Do this in writing, and keep a copy of the letter. Because you only have a 'reasonable' time from the date of delivery to reject your faulty car, time is of the essence.

There is no legal definition of a reasonable time, and it could include even the period before you had any inkling that the car was defective. In a 1986 case (Bernstein vs Pamson Motors) it was considered too late to reject a new car after only three weeks and 142 miles – even though the defect could not have been discovered earlier. However, the Sale of Goods Act 1979 was amended by the Sale and Supply of Goods Act 1994. Under amending legislation, the purchaser is not deemed to have accepted until he or she has had a 'reasonable opportunity of examining' the car. This could help consumers in similar cases in future by extending the purchaser's right to reject a car beyond the small amount of time permitted in the 1986 case described above.

If you don't reject the car in time, you are deemed to have 'accepted' it. This means that you are not entitled to get your money back. You are, however, entitled to recover compensation, which is usually assessed according to how much it will cost you to have the defect repaired.

If you allow a garage to repair the car you should make it clear that you are doing so 'without prejudice to my legal rights'. This means that you are reserving the right to claim from the dealer if the repair is unsuccessful. Under the amended Sale of Goods Act, the time that the car spends being repaired does not prejudice your right to reject the car within a 'reasonable' time. This advice also applies if you allow the dealer to repair the car under any guarantee provided at the time you bought the car.

A guarantee is additional to your legal rights – not instead of them. If you are covered by a guarantee and aren't entitled to reject the car and get your money back (because you had the car for too long) then the simplest and quickest way to get a repair may be under your guarantee.

Step three

If you are getting nowhere with your complaint and you intend to pursue the matter further, write to the seller again, stating a time limit for the problem to be sorted out and advising what action you will take if matters are not resolved.

Step four

If you need to take legal action, you should first make sure that you are suing the right person, and that whoever you are suing has enough funds to meet your claim. You should also check your evidence.

You will also need to consider which court procedure would be suitable for your sort of claim. If your claim is for £3,000 or less (£750 in Scotland) you can use the small claims procedure in the County Court. This is a simple, quick and cheap way of sorting out disputes where the amount involved is relatively small. You will have to pay an issue fee from £10 to £80, depending on the size of your claim. The hearing will be informal, without the formal rules for adducing of evidence. The services of a solicitor are not needed, and if you were unfortunate enough to lose you would only have to pay the other side's travel and witnesses' expenses. Details of the procedure are contained in an HMSO booklet, *Small Claims in the County Court*, which is available free of charge from all court offices.

The issue of a summons for more than £3,000 carries a lot of risk. In this case, the hearing would take place through the ordinary procedure of the County Court, which is very formal. Legal representation would be vital. If you were unlucky enough to lose, you would probably have to pay the other side's legal costs and witnesses' fees.

Alternatively, you could take your case to a trade association – assuming the trader belongs to one. The majority of car retailers belong to the Motor Agents Association (MAA),* the Scottish Motor Trade Association (SMTA),* or the Society of Motor Manufacturers and Traders (SMMT).*

These associations have jointly drawn up a Code of Practice for the motor industry in consultation with the Office of Fair Trading. The Code spells out the dealers' responsibilities to their customers and is backed up by a conciliation and arbitration service. If conciliation fails, and provided both parties agree, you can have the dispute referred to arbitration. Depending on the size of your claim you will be required to pay a fee. Your case will be heard by an independent arbitrator, whose decision will be final. Arbitration works on a documents-only basis. This means that you lose the impact of a verbal account of your troubles and have to match the written skill of the other side's professional advisers. You should bear in mind that if you choose to have the matter referred to arbitration you will lose your right to take the matter to court.

What if a car you bought privately is faulty or not as described?

Although it should be cheaper buying a car privately than through a dealer, the law doesn't give you as much protection. In private sales, the terms of the Sale of Goods Act (as amended), referring to satisfactory quality and fitness for purpose, do not apply. But the car should still correspond to the description applied to it in the advertisement, and any statements made about it must be correct.

So, if you are thinking of buying a car privately, you should get the car checked over properly first – see Chapter 5. It is also a good idea to ask lots of questions about the car that will give you the advantage of specific replies. The more the seller says, the stronger your position will be, especially if you are accompanied by a witness. And you should keep the advertisement if it contains a description of the car.

What if a car you bought at auction is faulty, or not as described?

Your rights are far weaker if you buy a car at auction. Not many people realise that when you buy a car at auction you are buying the car not from the auctioneer, but from the previous owner. This is because an auctioneer acts as agent to sell the car on behalf of its owner.

When you buy a car in this way you also agree to be bound by the auctioneer's terms and conditions of sale, although these are binding only in so far as they are fair and reasonable. You should always read these terms and conditions because some auctioneers undertake to give you your money back within a certain time limit if the car you have just bought turns out to be defective. Your rights under the auctioneer's terms and conditions of sale are particularly helpful if you can't trace the seller.

What if a car you are buying on credit is faulty?

If you finance the purchase of a car by entering into a regulated consumer credit agreement, you will have a dual weapon with which to fight the supplier or the creditor. The creditor is jointly liable with the supplier for breach of contract and/or misrepresentation. This is

67

laid down in the Consumer Credit Act 1974, and covers agreements where the cash price of the goods is between £100 and £30,000, and the amount of credit does not exceed £15,000.

THE LEGISLATION PROTECTING YOU

- The Supply of Goods (Implied Terms) Act 1973 (as amended) entitles you to a car that is of 'satisfactory quality', and the same Act also stipulates that the car should meet whatever description the seller has given of it.
- The Misrepresentation Act 1967 provides you with the right to back out of a contract and/or claim compensation if you can prove that you entered into the contract only through a false statement of fact by the supplier.
- The Trade Descriptions Act 1968 makes it a criminal offence to make false descriptions and statements about goods and services in the course of a trade or business.
- The Road Traffic Act 1972 (as amended) makes it an offence for anyone to sell a car that is unroadworthy without making it clear that it is only suitable for scrap.
- The Unfair Contract Terms Act 1977 regulates exclusion and limitation clauses, declaring that they are ineffective unless the person relying on them can show that they are fair and reasonable.
- The Unfair Terms in Consumer Contracts Regulations Act 1994, which supplements the Unfair Contract Terms Act 1977, ensures that terms that are 'unfair' are not enforceable against the consumer.

- The Consumer Credit Act 1974 makes the supplier of credit equally liable with the trader for defects in the goods.

LOOKING AFTER YOUR NEW CAR

8

Once you have bought a car, you should take steps to protect it from thieves. There are also ways to reduce the running costs that you will be liable for once you start to use the car.

CAR SECURITY

More and more car manufacturers are fitting security devices, such as alarms and immobilisers, to their cars. But it is still too easy for a thief to get into most cars and either steal the contents, or try to steal the car itself. There are more than a million victims of car crime each year – don't become one of them. There are steps that you can take to hinder thieves.

Staying secure

Always try to park in a well-lit, open area. A quarter of car crime occurs in car parks, so look for one that is well-supervised, well-lit and has restricted entry and exit points.

Don't leave anything on view in your car. You may know that what's in your car isn't very valuable, but a thief won't.

Make sure your car stereo is secure. Thieves are becoming increasingly knowledgeable about new security systems, so even security-coded radios are not totally immune. Coded units with a removable panel are a better choice. Stolen radios and phones are almost impossible to trace. So make life difficult for thieves – mark your radio or mobile phone with your car's registration number or VIN.

Fit security wheel bolts, especially if your car is fitted with alloy wheels. If your spare wheel is stowed under the car, make sure it's secure. This may mean fitting an extra lock.

Never leave documents, such as vehicle registration documents and MOT certificates, in the car. These can make it easier for a thief to sell the car. Don't leave anything with your name and address or signature on it inside the vehicle, as duplicate documents will be harder to obtain.

Extra protection

You may want to take extra steps to protect your car. A mechanical device, such as a steering-wheel lock, is the cheapest option, and may be enough to deter an opportunistic thief. An alarm or immobiliser is worth considering if you own a high-risk car or if you live in a high-risk area. Tracking devices can be useful to help locate a stolen car. If you discover that your car is missing, a phone call can activate the device. Some types emit a signal which can be picked up by police patrol cars. Others can actually pinpoint the position of the car.

Another option is vehicle watch schemes: these allow you to register your car, and mark it to say that it is not normally driven at certain times, or by drivers under a certain age. If police notice anything suspicious, they can check to see whether your car has been stolen.

RUNNING COSTS

Running a car isn't cheap, but there are savings to be made. The following pages contain a number of suggestions on how to cut your motoring costs without cutting corners.

Depreciation

This is the biggest single motoring cost for most people. The best way of reducing your depreciation costs is buying a second-hand car instead of a new one. The typical car will lose three-quarters of its value over a six-year period, including about 45 per cent in its first two years.

Also, some cars depreciate more than others. Cars which are predominantly bought for company use are particularly prone. Others, such as small cars or certain sought-after prestige makes, tend to hold their value well.

For example, a 1995 M-registration Ford Mondeo V6 Ghia automatic costs around £20,000 new, but within two years would have a trade-in value of less than £12,000 – a loss of more than £8,000. By contrast, an Audi A4 1.8 Turbo of the same age would have cost about the same new, but two years later would have a trade-in value of around £16,500 – a loss of only £3,500.

Factors such as the colour of the car or options fitted can also have an impact on resale value. Small cars fitted with power steering are always in demand, so they tend to keep their value well. As a general rule, the best bets are middle-range models rather than the most basic versions or expensive ones with all the trimmings. Special editions should be viewed with caution.

A snazzy paint job and customised interior will not guarantee that the car will hold its value – in fact, the reverse appears to be the case.

Fuel costs

Buying an economical car is better for the environment and will save you money. But, unless you do a high annual mileage, the savings will be suprisingly modest compared with your other motoring costs. If you do 10,000 miles a year, for example, annual fuel costs for a 35mpg car will be £790, compared with £550 for a 50mpg car.

Insurance

Car insurance costs can vary hugely from company to company, so shopping around could cut your car running costs considerably.

Your actual insurance costs will depend on a wide range of factors such as:

- your age
- your job
- your address
- your level of no-claims discount.

For more information on how to find the right type of insurance policy for your individual needs, see Chapter 1.

Servicing and repairs

This is another area where there are big price variations. If you have bought a car which is required to be serviced by a particular franchised dealer, you might think that all dealers specialising in the same make of car would charge the same amount for servicing and repairs. But *Which? Car** has found that costs can vary by up to 100 per cent for the same make and model of car. Travelling a bit further to get your car serviced may be inconvenient, but the savings could make it worthwhile.

Alternatively, you could use an independent garage for your servicing instead. Independents typically cost about two-thirds as much as franchised dealers. Always ask them to service your car according to the maker's schedule, and keep the service book up to date. This will enhance the value of the car when selling it.

If any faults or problems develop between regular services, get them looked at promptly. A relatively minor fault can develop into a major problem, possibly resulting in costly breakdowns.

Weekly maintenance

Keeping your car in good running order will help to prevent unexpected breakdowns and extend the life of the vehicle. Carry out the weekly checks as advised by the manufacturer. These include:

- engine oil level
- coolant level
- brake fluid level
- power steering fluid level
- screen washer fluid level
- battery condition and fluid level
- tyre pressures and condition (including the spare).

Clean and wash your car regularly, and from time to time treat and touch up any paint chips.

CHOOSING A CAR IF YOU HAVE SPECIAL NEEDS

Choosing the right car is a hard enough task. But for people who have a disability – anything from stiffness brought on by age, to using a wheelchair – the task is even harder. Paying a good price, or finding a car with the features you want, may be less important to you than finding a car you can get in and out of, or one which has controls within easy reach. Perhaps you are able-bodied yourself but have elderly parents or relatives whose mobility is limited, in which case certain factors could affect the type of car you choose.

MONEY MATTERS

If you have impaired mobility, you may be eligible for various benefits. Financial assistance is available to help you buy, run or sell a car. Contact your local Social Security office if you want to find out if you are entitled to any benefits because of a disability, or try the special free Benefit enquiry line* for disabled people and their carers.

There are two benefits specifically for people who are 'mobility-impaired':

- **Mobility Component of the Disability Living Allowance (DLA)** If you cannot walk very far, you may be eligible for this. Claims must be lodged before you reach the age of 66 and be for conditions which appeared before you were 65. However, once you have the allowance, it continues beyond the age of 66. There are two rates.

- **War Pensioners' Mobility Supplement (WPMS)** If you have a walking difficulty caused by a war disability you may be eligible for War Pensioners' Mobility Supplement. There is no upper age limit. You can't claim the WPMS and the Mobility Component of the Disability Living Allowance at the same time. Information about this benefit, including details of current rates, can be obtained from the War Pension Helpline.*

Motability

Motability* operates car finance schemes which make it easier for disabled people who qualify for the higher rate of the Disability Living Allowance or War Pensioners' Mobility Supplement to pay for both new and second-hand cars. Hire purchase can be used for second-hand cars, as long as they are bought from approved dealers and are under five years old with less than 60,000 miles on the clock. You must get a second-hand car inspected by the AA* too, and can only spread payments over two or three years. Motability can also provide grants to help with the cost of adapting your car.

Road tax

If you receive the higher-rate mobility component of

the Disability Living Allowance or the War Pensioners' Mobility Supplement, you don't have to pay road tax. This can be claimed only if the vehicle is used solely by or only for the purposes of carrying the disabled person concerned. The vehicle must be registered in the name of this person, or in the name of a driver they have nominated. See explanatory leaflet V188 or get further advice from DVLA Customer Enquiries Unit,* otherwise contact the Mobility Advice and Vehicle Information Service (MAVIS).*

Insurance

If you become disabled or have certain illnesses, some insurance companies may refuse to cover you or ask for an inflated premium. This is by no means the case with all companies, so shop around to find the best price. RICA* keeps comparative quotes of insurance for disabled drivers.

Roadside assistance

The AA,* RAC* and National Breakdown* all offer special roadside assistance and recovery for disabled motorists.

YOUR NEEDS

You should consider your requirements carefully and think about what situations you will encounter when using a car.

- Will you be driver, passenger or both?
- Will you travel independently, or will there be someone to help?
- If you drive by yourself, will you need any equip-

ment to help you get in and out?

- Will you carry bulky aids, such as a wheelchair, in the car? If so, how will you stow them?
- Will a standard car suit you, or will you have to consider adaptations?

The answers to these questions are likely to affect the features you need to look for and the car you choose. RICA* produces a range of publications that help you to assess your individual needs and offer practical advice, while the Mobility Advice and Vehicle Information Service MAVIS* publishes a free guide to 21 assessment centres around the UK that can advise you on your ability to drive and the type of equipment that might help you. These centres offer a personal appraisal of your needs and ability (which you must pay for), and some have adapted cars and equipment for you to see and try out.

It is also worth looking at car test reports in magazines such as *Autocar, Which?* and *What Car?*, which in addition often cover the special features and optional extras available in cars. Armed with this information, you should be able to draw up a shortlist of cars.

CHECKLIST

Before buying a car, you should put any vehicle that you are seriously considering through the following test.

Getting into the car

As you do this, think carefully about each of the following.

79

Unlocking the door

- Is remote locking available?
- Are keys easy to grip?

Door handles

Some car door handles are much more difficult to use than others.

- Are they comfortable to grasp?
- Can you operate them easily?

The door

Some car doors are much stiffer and heavier than others. Don't assume they will get easier with age.

- Can you move the door easily? You may need to open it on a hill or in a strong wind.
- Does it open far enough for you?

Once you have got the door open, consider the best way of getting on to the seat. Whatever method of getting in you use:

- Check that seats can be pushed far back enough if you need a lot of space to bring your legs in. Can you recline the seat back easily?
- Check that any pocket on the inside of the door won't get in the way. Would it make any difference if it was removed?
- Think about where you will stow any mobility aids that you will use.
- If you slide across from the passenger side, do the hand brake (when fully engaged), gear stick or selector get in the way?

Handholds and supports

Look for the best places to hold on to as you get in. Try varying your technique – you may find that small changes make a big difference. Unless you fit them yourself, you will rarely find handles where you want them. Think what handholds and supports you might be able to use, and in what order. Make sure that anything you want to grasp or lean on will take your weight. Check for sharp edges.

When first getting into the car, try to see if any of these commonly used handholds might be acceptable for you.

- parts of the door, including the window sill
- parts of the car body – around the door space, including the roof gutter if the car has one
- interior handles or arm-rests on the door
- the seat or its back rest – check that the upholstery is firm and durable
- an open sun roof.

If the steering wheel or any other obstacle gets in the way, you may have to consider another car.

Further inside the car, you may have to transfer your weight to other supports, so try:

- the steering-wheel
- the dashboard
- the seat or its back rest
- any grab handle above the door

Sills

- Is the sill low enough to the ground?

- Is the sill low enough to the car floor?
- Might you catch your heel or toe, or callipers (if you wear them) on the sill?

Inside the car

Once you have got into the car, you will have a different set of considerations.

The seat

Sit in the seat for a good while to get an idea of comfort. Remember that the height of the seat in relation to the ground will be different depending on how high the kerb is.

- Is the seat the right height?
- Does its shape cause problems for you?
- Is it hard enough? Soft edges can be dangerous if you need to sit on them when getting in or out.

Adjusting the seat

If you are likely to make frequent adjustments, look closely at the controls. Generally, levers should be large and thick (hence easier to grip) and should not be too stiff. Round knobs should not have smooth edges (which makes them harder to turn). The larger they are, the better.

Drivers often hold on to the steering wheel to give some leverage when pulling the seat forward. This is not possible on the passenger side, so look for (and try grasping) any corresponding feature on the dashboard. Avoid the combination of a seat which is stiff to move and a completely smooth dashboard, particularly if you are unable to brace your feet against the floor.

- Can you reach the controls you will use?
- Can you grasp and operate them comfortably?
- Do the controls move easily and stop where you want them to?
- Do other parts of the car get in the way?
- Will you still be able to reach and use the controls once any equipment you normally carry with you is in the car?
- When adjusting the seat, do you need to pull against anything with the other hand? Is there a convenient handhold?

Seat belts

You have to turn and stretch at the same time to reach seat belts. This is especially true in two-door cars because the seat belt mounting points may be placed well behind the seat. After you have adjusted the seat to suit you, adjust the position of the mounting point, if it is available. Then try putting on and taking off the seat belt, considering the following questions:

- How easy is it to turn and reach for it?
- Can you pull the belt across your body? Some have a strong spring.
- Is it difficult to locate the socket and plug the belt into it? Sockets mounted on flexible stalks are often more difficult to cope with than fixed ones.
- Does the belt sit comfortably across your body, in particular across your lower neck and shoulders?

Closing the door
- Can you reach the door handle from the seat and pull the door shut?
- It may help to use a hooked stick or a length of cord.

Stowing wheelchairs and other aids

Mobility aids need to be stored safely and so that they are accessible.

Walking sticks and crutches
Walking sticks and crutches are often stowed on the back seat, or alongside either side of the front seat – try these options out. Walking frames are sometimes bulky and it can be awkward to get them on to the back seat of a two-door car without help. Consider getting one that folds up.

Stowing a wheelchair in the boot or hatch
It can be a considerable strain to lift a wheelchair into the boot or hatch of a car. The height of the rear sill, the distance you have to stretch over the back bumper, and the dimension of the boot all vary greatly from car to car. If you need help with this, the person who normally helps you out should try out the car too. A strap or cord may help you close the hatch.

- Check that anything you are likely to carry regularly fits in reasonably easily.
- Check you can close the boot or hatch afterwards.

Stowing a wheelchair behind the front seats
- Can you move the seat forward and backwards easily?

- Is there enough clearance behind the seat?
- Do seat-belt anchorage points get in the way?
- Is there a bulky transmission tunnel in the rear?
- Is the door sill shallow enough?

Getting out of the car

The difficulties involved in getting out of the car are similar to the difficulties getting in, so most of them have already been covered.

Seat belts
- How easy is it to release the seat-belt buckle?
- Does it retract too quickly?

The door
- Is the door catch easy to use?
- Is the door light enough to push open?
- Will the door stay open?

The seat
You may need to move the seat back as far as it will go while you are sitting in it – so that you have enough space to swing your legs out, or because you need to get a walking aid out of the car before you get up from the seat.

- Can you reach and use the lever which moves the seat forward and back while sitting in it?
- Does the seat move easily when you are sitting in it?
- Can you reach the handle which adjusts the angle of the bracket easily while sitting in the seat?
- Can you grasp it and use it comfortably while sitting?

- Does the back rest move easily and stop where you want it to?

Getting up

Most people find it more difficult to get up from the seat than to get into it. It takes some effort to push yourself up from a low seat and you need to be able to bend your knees and hips.

- Is there enough room to swing your legs out?
- Is the door sill low and flat enough to swing your legs over?
- Is the seat high enough?
- Is the seat level enough and without bulky wings?

Handholds and supports

In addition to those you may have used when getting in, try:

- the seat-back
- the sill.

Getting in and out of a car easily is often a matter of using the right technique. RICA* can provide further information on the best way to fit yourself, plus your wheelchair and any other mobility aids if applicable, into a car.

FEATURES TO LOOK OUT FOR

You should think about buying a car equipped with specifications designed to make life easier. Today there are a large number of features available that ensure a high level of comfort, particularly in the more recent models.

- Automatic transmission and power-assisted steering save a lot of effort and mean that you are less likely to get tired.
- Central locking, cruise control, electronically operated windows and exterior mirrors may also save effort.
- Adjustable seats that let you alter the lumbar support can make a great deal of difference to your comfort.

ADAPTING YOUR CAR

A wide range of adaptations and add-on devices are available to make getting in and out easier for people who are elderly or disabled. Many also improve your driving capability and in-car comfort.

The main types of aids available include the following devices.

- Lightweight moulded plastic handles can be added to keys to make gripping easier and give better leverage.
- Car door handles and catches may be too stiff or awkward if you have a weak grip or limited movement. Various devices are available to help you operate door handles and catches.
- Interior handholds can be fitted that you lean on when getting in or out of the car.
- Struts can be fitted to hold the door in place if it is important that it does not move when you are getting in and out.
- A leg lifter may help you lift your legs over the door sill more easily (you could try using a hooked walking stick).

- Runners could be added to the car seat if you need to move it further forwards or backwards than the manufacturer intended.
- Swivelling seats turn 90° to face out of the car; some slide over the sill, too. They make it easier for you to turn round (though not to stand up).
- Swivelling cushions can be added to a normal seat to make the seat higher and help you to turn.
- Height-adjustable seats are electrically operated, and may be a standard fitting or an optional extra.
- Seats to help you stand up are available. These are powered by car battery.
- The steering wheel may get in the way of your knees. On some cars, it can be modified to give you more room.
- Seat-belt accessories are available for those who do not have full use of their hands or find standard seat belts uncomfortable.

RICA* can provide more information on the type of aids currently available and how to obtain them.

SAFETY MATTERS

Don't forget the safety aspects. When driving or travelling in a car, you must make sure that what you do is legal, and that you are not at greater risk of injury than any other motorist.

Seat belts
You have to use a seat belt by law. You could investigate seat-belt adaptations (above). If you are unable to

wear one, see your doctor about an exemption certificate (but consider this only as a last resort).

Travelling in a wheelchair

If travelling *in* your wheelchair, make sure it is safely anchored to the car using a wheelchair tie-down system. You should also have a special seat belt or harness which is anchored to the vehicle. Belts fitted to wheelchairs as postural supports are both illegal and unsafe – you should not rely on these. Take advice from equipment manufacturers about which system to use with your wheelchair.

Stowing aids

Unless you store any aids you travel with in an enclosed boot, you should strap them down. Check that moving parts of any equipment, such as hoists, are secured before you drive off.

ADDRESSES

AA
(0990) 500600 *(general information)*
(0800) 444999 *(membership enquiries)*
(0800) 234999 *(car check)*

Benefit Enquiry Line
(0800) 882200
(0800) 220674 *(Northern Ireland)*
(0800) 243355 *(Minicom)*

CCN
(0800) 234999

Driver Vehicle and Licensing Authority (DVLA)
Swansea SA99 1BL
(01792) 772134 *(general information)*

HPI Register
(01722) 422422

Institute of Automotive Engineer Assessors
Stowe House, Netherstowe,
Lichfield, Staffordshire WS13 6TJ
(01543) 251346

Insurance Ombudsman Bureau (IOB)
General Enquiries,
City Gate 1, 135 Park Street,
London SE1 9EA
0171-928 7600

Mobility Advice and Vehicle Information Service (MAVIS)
O Wing, Macadam Avenue,
Old Wokingham Road, Crowthorne,
Berkshire RG45 6XD
(01344) 661000

Motability
Goodman House, Station Approach,
Harlow, Essex CM20 2ET
(01279) 635666

Motor Agents Association (MAA)
201 Great Portland Street, London W1N 6AB
0171-580 9122

National Breakdown
PO Box 300, Leeds LS99 2LZ
0113-239 3666

Personal Insurance Arbitration Service (PIAS)
24 Angel Gate, City Road,
London EC1V 2RS
0171-837 4483

RAC
(0990) 722722 *(general information)*
(0990) 333660 *(car check)*

RICA (Research Institute for Consumer Affairs)
2 Marylebone Road, London NW1 4DF
0171-830 6000 *(general information)*
This charity focuses on research for elderly and disabled consumers and publishes several motoring guides for this market

Scottish Motor Trade Association (SMTA)
3 Palmerston Place, Edinburgh EH12 5AF
0131-225 3643

Society of Motor Manufacturers and Traders (SMMT)
Forbes House, Halkin Street,
London SW1X 7DX
0171-235 7000

War Pension Helpline
(01253) 858858

Which? Car
PO Box 44, Hertford X, SG14 1SH
(0800) 252100 *(Which? subscriptions)*
An annual supplement issued free of charge to Which? *subscribers*

INDEX

Other titles in this series

Buying a Computer
Buy the system that's right for you, and don't be intimidated by the technical jargon. This guide explains how to make the right decisions, how to keep your information safe, how to get help when you need it, and much more.

Making Money at Home
You can earn money without the daily grind of commuting, even if you are tied to the home by young children. This book describes some of the opportunities available and tells you what you need to consider before you get started.

You and Your Doctor
Ever felt that there's an unnecessary barrier between you and your GP? This book explains what you are entitled to expect from your doctor and how to get the best health care from the NHS in general and your GP's practice in particular.

Safe as Houses
Don't become a crime statistic! Check out the security of your home using this book and you'll be able to tip the odds against the burglar.

Countdown to Moving House
Buying and selling property, and moving itself, are stressful activities. Stay in control and leave nothing to chance by using this book's tips and checklists.

Here's just a flavour of some of the reports planned for future issues of *Which?*

- Multimedia PCs on test • Tumble driers • Stereo systems
- Compact cameras • Current accounts • Claiming on car insurance
- Health insurance • Shopping on the Internet • Washing machines
- Large family cars • Postal deliveries • Council Tax
- Package holidays • Credit reference agencies • Best Buy PEPs

So why not take up our trial offer today?

SUMMARY OF OFFER

3 free issues of Which? as they are published • Just fill in the delayed direct debiting instruction below and post it to Which?, FREEPOST, Hertford X, SG14 1YB • If you do not wish to continue beyond the free trial period write to us at the address above, and to your Bank/Building Society to cancel your direct debiting instruction, before the 1st payment is due • You first payment will be due on the 1st of the month 3 months after the date you sign the mandate (so for example, if you sign the mandate on 15th August, your 1st payment is due on 1st November) • No action is necessary if you wish to continue after the free trial. We will send you Which? each month for the current price of £14.75 a quarter, until you cancel or until we advise you of a change in price • We would give you at least 6 weeks notice in advance of any change in price, so you would have plenty of time to decide whether to continue – you are of course free to cancel at any time.

Offer subject to acceptance. Which? Ltd, Reg in England Reg No 677665. Reg Office 2 Marylebone Road, London NW1 4DF. Reg under the Data Protection Act. As result of responding to this offer, your name and address might be added to a mailing list. This could be used by ourselves (Which? Ltd, or our parent company Consumers' Association) or other companies for sending you offers in the future. If you prefer not to receive such offers, please write to Dept DNP3 at the above Hertford address or tick the box on the coupon if you only want to stop offers from other companies. You will not be sent any future offers for 5 years, in compliance with the British Code of Advertising and Sales Promotion.

▼ DETACH HERE ▼

Your name and address in BLOCK CAPITALS PLEASE

Name (Mr/Mrs/Miss/Ms)	Address	
		Postcode

To: Which?, FREEPOST, Hertford X, SG14 1YB
Please send me the next 3 months' issues of Which? magazine as they appear. I understand that I am under no obligation – if I do not wish to continue after the 3 months' free trial, I can cancel my order before my first payment is due on the 1st of the month 3 months after the date I sign the mandate. But if I decide to continue I need do nothing – my subscription will bring me monthly Which? for the current price of £14.75 a quarter.

Direct Debiting Instruction Please pay Which? Ltd Direct Debits from the account detailed on this Instruction subject to the safeguards assured by The Direct Debit Guarantee. I understand that this Instruction may remain with Which? and if so, details will be passed electronically to any bank or building society.

Signed	Date

Bank/Building Society account in the name of	Name and address of your Bank/Building Society in BLOCK CAPITALS PLEASE

*Banks/Building Societies may decline to accept Direct Debits to certain types of account other than current accounts

*Bank/Building Society Acct. No.

Bank/Building Society Sort Code

Tick here if you do not wish to receive promotional mailings from other companies ☐

To:

Postcode

NO STAMP NEEDED • SEND NO MONEY